THE ELEMENTS

Lithium

Tom Jackson

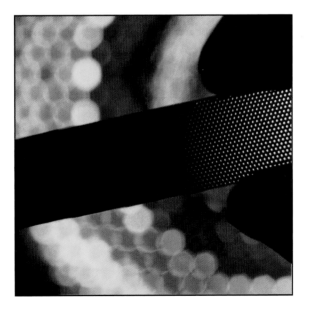

Marshall Cavendish
Benchmark

New York

Marshall Cavendish Benchmark
99 White Plains Road
Tarrytown, New York 10591

www.marshallcavendish.us

Library of Congress Cataloging-in-Publication Data

Jackson, Tom, 1972–
Lithium / Tom Jackson.
p.   cm – (The elements)
Includes index.
ISBN-13: 978-0-7614-2199-3
ISNB-10: 0-7614-2199-8
1. Lithium—Juvenile literature. 2. Chemical elements—Juvenile literature. I. Title. II.
Elements (Marshall Cavendish Benchmark)
QD181.L5J33   2007
546'.381—dc22

2005055302

1 6 5 4 3 2

Printed in Malaysia

Picture credits
Front cover: 2004 RGB Research Ltd.
Back cover: Photos.com

2004 RGB Research Ltd.: www.element-collection.com 14
Stan Celestian: 12
Corbis: 23, Lester V. Bergman 3, 6, José Manuel Sanchis Calvete 11, Charles O'Rear 1, 20
Ecoscene: Alan Towse 30
NASA: Marrin Smith/GRC 24
Photos.com: 7, 25
Science Photo Library: Andrew Lambert Photography 8, Martyn F. Chillmaid 4, 18,
Custom Medical Stock Photo 27, Laguna Design 9, NASA 21, Charles D. Winters 16
University of Pennsylvania Library: Edgar Fahs Smith Collection 5, 10

Series created by The Brown Reference Group plc.
Designed by Sarah Williams
www.brownreference.com

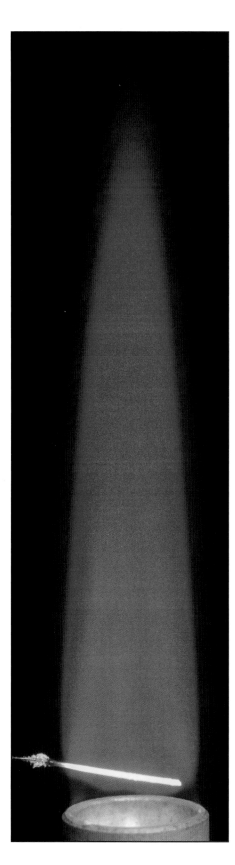

Contents

What is lithium?

Lithium is a white, shiny metal. It is very light—so light that it will float on water. Lithium is also very soft compared to most metals. For example, solid lithium can be cut into slices using a sharp steel knife.

Lithium belongs to a group of elements called the alkali metals. The alkali metals are among the most reactive of all elements.

Lithium atoms

Everything in the universe consists of tiny particles called atoms. Atoms are the building blocks of all the elements.

Lithium is one of about ninety elements that exist in nature. The atoms of each element are uniquely structured. It is the structure of its atoms that makes an element look and behave the way it does.

Atoms are very small—far too small even to be seen with the most powerful microscopes. The period at the end of this sentence would cover 250 billion atoms.

Atoms themselves are made from even smaller particles. At the center of an atom is a nucleus. The nuclei in the atoms of

Most of this piece of lithium is covered in a dark coating. This forms as the lithium reacts with the oxygen in the air. The shiny surface has just been cut so it has not had time to tarnish, or become dull.

nearly all elements are made up of two types of particles called protons and neutrons. (A hydrogen atom is unusual because it has just one proton in its nucleus and no neutrons.) Protons are positively charged particles. Neutrons do not have a charge—they are neutral. Lithium atoms have three protons in their nucleus. Most of them also have four neutrons.

Atomic number

The number of protons in an atom is called the atomic number. Lithium has three protons, so its atomic number is three. All other elements have a different atomic number. For example, hydrogen has an atomic number of one, while uranium has an atomic number of 92.

The number of protons and neutrons in an atom's nucleus is called the atomic mass number. In the case of most lithium atoms, this is three protons plus four neutrons, making an atomic mass number of seven. However, some lithium atoms only have three neutrons, so they have an atomic mass number of just six.

Both types of atoms are still lithium because they have three protons. Chemists refer to the different version of lithium atoms as isotopes. About 19 out of every 20 lithium atoms are the lithium-7 isotope. The others are lithium-6. The average atomic mass number of all lithium atoms put together is 6.9.

DID YOU KNOW?

ORIGIN OF THE NAME LITHIUM

Lithium was given its name because it was first found inside a rock. The name *lithium* comes from the Greek word *lithos*, which means "stone." Lithium was named by its discoverer Swedish chemist Johan August Arfwedson (1792–1841). He added "-ium" to *lithos* to show that the new element was a metal. Literally, lithium means "stone metal." Arfwedson did not know what pure lithium looked like. However, he did know that it was an alkali metal. The two other alkali metals known at the time—potassium and sodium—were first found in plants and were named for those sources.

When pure lithium was produced many years later, it turned out that the metal was nothing like rock. Most stones are heavy and hard, but pure lithium is a very light and soft substance.

Johan August Arfwedson

Electrons

An atom's nucleus is surrounded by other particles called electrons. These are much smaller than the particles in the nucleus. Electrons have a negative charge. Opposite charges attract each other, and the negatively charged electrons are held close to the nucleus by the positively charged protons inside.

The number of electrons in an atom is always the same as the number of protons in the atom. Therefore, lithium atoms have three electrons moving around the nucleus.

Even though it is more than a thousand times smaller than a proton, the charge of an electron is equal to the charge of a proton. Therefore, the electrons' negative charges cancel out the positive charges of the protons. This make the whole lithium atom neutral.

Shells

Electrons move around the nucleus a little like planets moving around the Sun. The electrons are arranged in layers called electron shells. Lithium has two electron shells. The first shell has two electrons in it. This shell has no more room for another electron, so the third electron is in the

When lithium metal is heated it burns with a bright red flame. Chemists look for this color in flames to see if the substance being burned contains lithium.

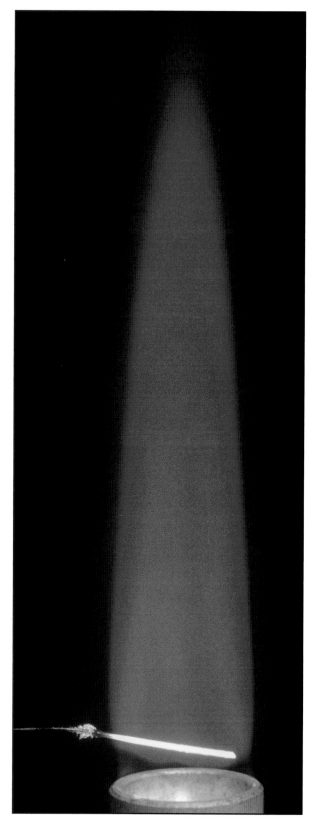

LITHIUM ATOM

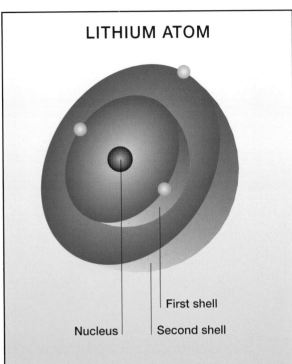

First shell

Nucleus

Second shell

The number of positively charged protons in the nucleus of an atom is balanced by the number of negatively charged electrons outside the nucleus. A lithium atom contains three electrons. These orbit the nucleus in two layers, or shells. There are two electrons in the inner shell and one in the outer shell.

second shell, slightly farther away from the nucleus. The second shell has room for a total of eight electrons.

Atoms are most stable if their shells are full. To become stable, atoms will find ways of emptying or filling their outer shells. This is what drives reactions. In reactions, atoms gain, lose, or share their outer electrons. As they react, atoms of different elements combine to form compounds.

Lithium has only one electron to lose to make it stable. It is much easier to give away just one electron during a chemical reaction than it is to lose two or three. Because of this, lithium forms compounds more easily than most other elements.

The red color in fireworks is caused by lithium compounds. The explosive in the firework burns the lithium compounds causing the colored flash.

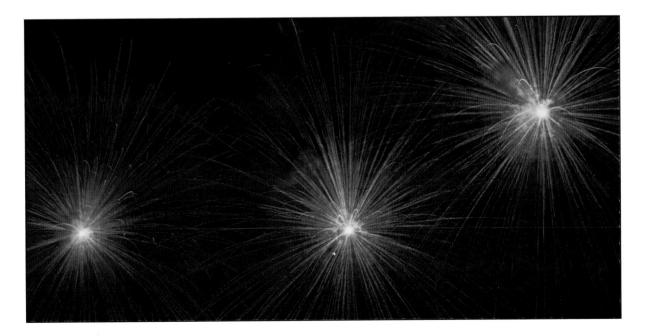

Special characteristics

A small piece of lithium reacts with water. Because of its low density, the solid lithium floats. The reaction between the water and lithium produces bubbles of hydrogen gas.

Lithium is the least dense of all solid elements. Density is a measure of how heavy a set amount of a substance is. For example, lithium is much less dense than iron, so a handful of lithium weighs a lot less than one of iron. Lithium is also almost half as dense as water.

Empty space

Lithium is very light because it has a small and simple atom. Only hydrogen and helium atoms are simpler than lithium. Lithium is a solid in normal conditions.

Inside the solid, atoms are stacked in a repeating pattern called a crystal lattice. Each atom in the lattice is surrounded by eight other atoms.

A lithium atom takes up more room than a hydrogen or helium atom because it has one more electron shell. However, most of the outer shell is empty of electrons, so the lithium atom takes up a large space considering the weight of the few particles inside it.

LITHIUM FACTS

- Chemical symbol: Li
- Atomic number: 3
- Atomic mass number: 6.9 (average)
- Melting point: 356 °F (180 °C)
- Boiling point: 2447 °F (1342 °C)
- Density: 0.53 g/cm^3.
  (0.53 times the density of water.)

Because lithium is so light, it is used for making strong but lightweight alloys. An alloy is a mixture of metals. Lithium-containing alloys are used to make aircraft.

Staying cool

Lithium also has the highest specific heat of any element. Specific heat is a measure of how much heat is needed to raise 0.035 ounce (1 g) of a substance by 1.8 °F (1 °C). Some materials, such as copper, warm up very quickly. They have a low specific heat. On the other hand, lithium has to be heated a long time to make its temperature go up.

Because of this, lithium is often used to make efficient heat-transfer systems. The energy flows straight through the lithium and is not wasted by heating it. For

Inside solid lithium, the atoms are stacked in a repeating pattern described as body centered cubic. Each atom is at the center of a cube made up of eight other atoms.

example, some nuclear reactors use melted lithium to carry the heat produced by nuclear fuel out of the reactor.

Heat and temperature are not quite the same thing. The atoms inside an object are always moving slightly. If the object gets hotter, the atoms move more. The energy that makes the atoms move is transferred from atom to atom as heat. Heat always moves from hot objects to cooler ones.

Temperature is a measure of how much heat energy the atoms in an object have. With their high specific heat, lithium atoms do not absorb much of the heat energy flowing through the metal. Therefore most of the energy passes through the lithium, and only a small amount of energy makes the atoms move.

History of lithium

Lithium was discovered by Swedish chemist Johan August Arfwedson in 1817. He was analyzing a sample of petalite, a mineral collected from a remote Swedish island. (A mineral is a compound that occurs naturally. Rocks are mixtures of several minerals.)

Arfwedson showed that the mineral contained an element that behaved in the same way as sodium and potassium. He suggested that this element was a new but similar element. Today chemists know that petalite is a complex compound containing aluminum, silicon, oxygen, and lithium.

Humphry Davy was the first person to isolate pure lithium. He used a powerful electric battery to separate the lithium from its compounds.

DISCOVERERS

Johan August Arfwedson was the son of a wealthy merchant. By the time he was twenty years old, Arfwedson has already completed two college degrees. He trained as a lawyer, but was also an expert in minerals. He began to work for the Swedish government helping to organize the mines in the country. In 1817, Arfwedson then went to work for the famous Swedish chemist Jöns Jacob Berzelius (1779–1848). It was in Berzelius's laboratory that Arfwedson discovered lithium in the mineral petalite. However, he was unable to purify this new element. The rare mineral arvedsonite, which also contains lithium, was later named for Arfwedson.

Pure metal

Arfwedson was unable to isolate pure lithium. However, this was done soon after lithium was discovered. English chemist and inventor Humphry Davy (1778–1829) used electricity to break lithium chloride (LiCl) into separate atoms. Ten years earlier, Davy had used the same technique to isolate pure sodium and potassium. The method he used is called electrolysis, which means "splitting with electricity." Lithium is still purified by electrolysis today.

Lithium in nature

Pure lithium metal is never found in nature. Lithium is much too reactive for this. Instead lithium combines with other elements to form many natural compounds, or minerals. Most of the time lithium is combined with silicon, phosphorus, and oxygen.

Big crystals

Lithium is a rare element. Only 1 out of 10 million atoms in seawater is a lithium atom. The metal also makes up only 0.002 percent of the elements in Earth's rocky crust. Lithium is more common in hot liquid rock, called magma. Most of the time, magma is deep underground. Sometimes it rises closer to Earth's surface, where it cools into solid rock.

Most lithium-rich minerals are found in rocks that have formed from magma that cooled slowly. This makes rock, such as granite, that is made up of large crystals.

Lithium minerals

The most common lithium mineral is called lepidolite. This forms pink or purple minerals, which are common in some types of granite. Lepidolite belongs to a large group of flaky minerals called micas. It is sometimes called lithia mica. Another important lithium-containing mineral is amblygonite. This is a phosphate mineral that also contains sodium and aluminum. Amblygonite is found in granite, often in white lumps.

A polished nodule of kunzite.

How lithium is made

Lithium is a reactive metal and forms compounds easily. This makes it hard to purify because once the lithium atoms have been taken out of one compound, they quickly form another. Chemical reactions are not used to isolate pure lithium. Instead lithium is purified by electrolysis.

Lepidolite is one of the main lithium ores. It also contains other metals, such as potassium, aluminum, silicon, and fluorine.

Lithium ores

An ore is a mineral or rock that contains a useful amount of an important substance. The main lithium ores are lepidolite, spodumene, and amblygonite. However, because lithium is rare, even its ores only contain a small amount of the element. Most lithium ores contain between 4 and 8 percent lithium. Most lithium compounds dissolve in water, and some spring waters are rich in the metal.

For example, the water in Searles Lake in California contains a lot of lithium oxide (Li_2O).

Chemical preparation

Pure lithium is made by electrolyzing melted lithium chloride (LiCl). The main method for making lithium chloride begins with the ore being heated to drive off any water molecules locked away in its crystals. Then the dry crystals are added to sulfuric acid (H_2SO_4). This creates a violent reaction in which lithium sulfate (Li_2SO_4) is formed. Any acid left over in the mixture is removed by adding calcium

---

DID YOU KNOW?

Lithium chloride can be made by reacting lithium gas with either hydrogen chloride gas (HCl) or pure chlorine gas (Cl_2). The ore is broken up into a powder and heated up. This is done by adding it to burning coal or using an electric furnace. At high temperature the gases can react with the lithium atoms locked away inside the ore.

carbonate ($CaCO_3$). This produces calcium sulfate ($CaSO_4$) from the remaining acid. Unlike lithium sulfate, calcium sulfate does not dissolve. Instead it sinks to the bottom as a white powder. This leaves a solution of lithium sulfate. (When a substance dissolves, it mixes in with a liquid so completely that it disappears. A liquid containing a dissolved substance is called a solution.)

The dissolved lithium sulfate is converted into lithium carbonate by adding sodium carbonate ($NaCO_3$). The sodium replaces the lithium in the sulfate compound. This reaction works this way because sodium is more reactive than lithium. Most of the lithium compounds people need can be made from lithium carbonate, including the lithium chloride used for electrolysis.

Electric current

Before the electrolysis begins, the lithium chloride is mixed with potassium chloride (KCl). This mixture melts into a liquid at about 752 °F (400 °C), a lower temperature than pure lithium chloride. Electrolysis also works best at this temperature.

When lithium chloride is formed, a lithium atom gives its single outer electron to the chlorine atom. Without the electron, the lithium atom becomes a positively charged lithium ion (Li^+). The chlorine turns into a negatively charged

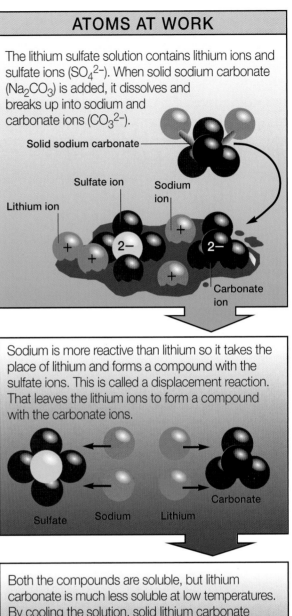

ATOMS AT WORK

The lithium sulfate solution contains lithium ions and sulfate ions (SO_4^{2-}). When solid sodium carbonate (Na_2CO_3) is added, it dissolves and breaks up into sodium and carbonate ions (CO_3^{2-}).

Solid sodium carbonate
Sulfate ion
Sodium ion
Lithium ion
Carbonate ion

Sodium is more reactive than lithium so it takes the place of lithium and forms a compound with the sulfate ions. This is called a displacement reaction. That leaves the lithium ions to form a compound with the carbonate ions.

Sulfate
Sodium
Lithium
Carbonate

Both the compounds are soluble, but lithium carbonate is much less soluble at low temperatures. By cooling the solution, solid lithium carbonate forms and sinks to the bottom.

Solid lithium carbonate
Sodium ions
Sulfate ion

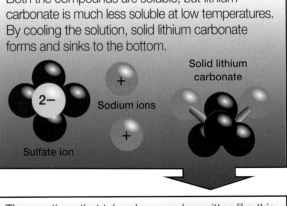

The reactions that take place can be written like this:
$$Li_2SO_4 + Na_2CO_3 \rightarrow Li_2CO_3 + Na_2SO_4$$

chloride ion (Cl⁻). Because opposite charges are attracted to each other, these two ions bond together. Lithium chloride crystals contain many ions stuck together.

Once it is melted, the ions in the liquid lithium chloride are no longer rigidly stuck to each other. Instead they are free to move around. This allows an electric current to pass through the liquid.

Back to atoms

Electrolysis involves a large electric current passing through a liquid between two terminals, or electrodes. The liquid is called the electrolyte. In this case, the electrolyte is the melted chloride mixture.

<table>
<tr><td colspan="2">LITHIUM FACTS</td></tr>
<tr><td colspan="2">Production of pure lithium in 2003.</td></tr>
<tr><td>● Chile</td><td>5,920 tons (5,730 tonnes)</td></tr>
<tr><td>● Australia</td><td>3,140 tons (2,848 tonnes)</td></tr>
<tr><td>● China</td><td>2,400 tons (2,177 tonnes)</td></tr>
<tr><td>● Argentina</td><td>946 tons (858 tonnes)</td></tr>
<tr><td>● World total</td><td>14,200 tons (12,882 tonnes)</td></tr>
</table>

The United States does make some of its own lithium but also imports a lot of lithium from Chile.

When the electric current is turned on, electrons flow into the negative electrode. This is known as the cathode and is made of graphite carbon, similar to the material used in pencil leads. The cathode becomes negatively charged, and the positively charged lithium ions in the electrolyte move toward it.

The positive electrode, or anode, is being emptied of electrons. This makes it positively charged, and the negatively charged chloride ions move towards it.

To complete the circuit and keep the current flowing, electrons need to empty into the electrolyte from the cathode, and they need to flow from the electrolyte into the anode. Electrons on their own cannot move through the liquid very easily.

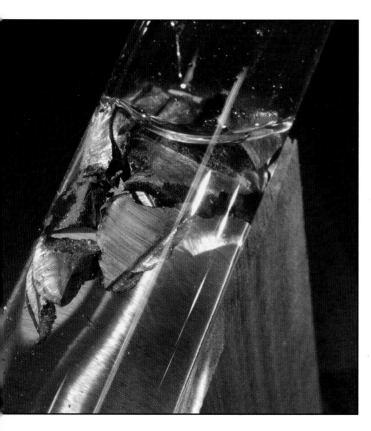

Pure lithium is too reactive to be stored in air because it reacts with the oxygen and moisture in it. Instead lithium is stored in oil, which stops it from reacting.

Instead the lithium ions pick up electrons from the cathode. This turns them back into lithium atoms with three electrons. At the same time, chloride ions each give up one electron at the anode. They then become chlorine atoms again. With the lithium ions taking electrons and the chlorine ions giving them away, the electric current continues to flow around the circuit.

Pure metal

As the lithium ions turn into lithium atoms, they form a pool of pure liquid lithium. This pool floats on top of the electrolyte surrounding the cathode. Even though the electrolyte also contains potassium ions, only the lithium ions are involved in the electrolysis. This is because the current is not strong enough to turn potassium ions into atoms. Therefore the lithium metal that forms is very pure.

Separating out

The lithium is scooped up and poured into a mold. The mold is kept at just above lithium's melting point. At this temperature, any electrolyte liquid that has also been scooped up turns into a solid and sinks to the bottom. This process makes lithium so pure that only 100 atoms out of every one million in the metal are not lithium atoms.

ATOMS AT WORK

The electrodes are dipped in a melted mixture of lithium chloride. Because the mixture is melted, the ions are free to move around.

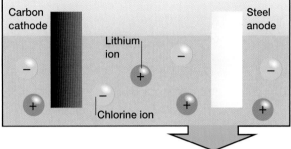

When the current is turned on, electrons flow to the cathode making it negative. Positive lithium ions are attracted toward the cathode. Negative chloride ions move to the anode which is now positively charged.

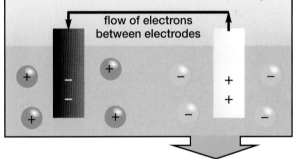

Electrons move from the cathode to the lithium ions, creating lithium atoms. A pool of pure lithium forms. Electrons from the chloride ions move to the anode. This turns them into chlorine atoms, which bubble out of the liquid as gas (Cl_2).

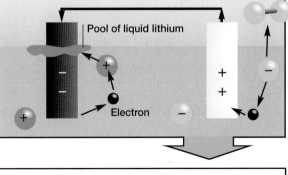

The reaction that takes place can be written like this:

$$2Li^+ + 2Cl^- \rightarrow 2Li + Cl_2$$

Chemistry and compounds

L ike all alkali metals, lithium is very reactive. It has just one electron in its outer shell. A lithium atom needs to lose the one electron in its outer shell before becoming stable. Chemists describe this behavior as being very electropositive. Electropositive elements are those that lose electrons and become positively charged ions. Lithium is one of the most electropositive elements.

Least reactive
All alkali metals have just one electron in their outer shell and they all react in the same way. Lithium is the least reactive of the alkali metals. (Francium is the most reactive alkali metal and it is also the rarest and most reactive of all metals.)

Lithium's reactivity is due to the size of its atoms. A lithium atom is the smallest of the alkali metals, with only two electron shells. Therefore, its outer electron is closer to the nucleus than in other alkali metals.

The positively charged nucleus pulls on the negatively charged electron. The pull of the nucleus is greater in lithium than in other, larger alkali-metal atoms. This makes it harder for the outer electron to break free from the lithium atom as it takes part in a chemical reactions. Atoms

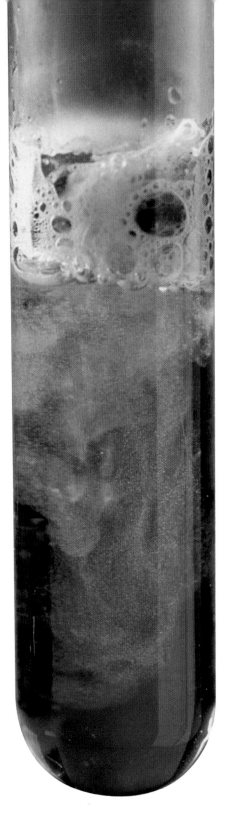

Lithium metal reacts with water in a test tube. The reaction produces lithium hydroxide and hydrogen gas.

that lose electrons easily react easily, too. For example, francium atoms have seven electron shells, so the nucleus only pulls on the outer electron with a very weak force. Francium atoms lose their outer electrons much more easily than lithium atoms, making francium more reactive.

Chemical bonds

Atoms take on more stable forms as a result of chemical reactions. Chemical reactions involve atoms of two or more elements combining to form compounds. The compound forms because the atoms are more stable in the compound than they were before combining.

There are two ways that a compound can form. Two atoms can share their outer electrons. Together, the atoms' outer electrons add up to a full, stable electron shell. Sharing the electrons makes the atoms cling together as a compound. This is called covalent bonding.

Lithium, however, rarely forms covalent bonds. Most lithium compounds are ionic. Instead of sharing electrons, lithium atoms give them away. Losing its outer electron, turns the lithium atom into an ion with a charge of +1. The lithium ion is more stable than the lithium atom because its one remaining electron shell is full.

The electron released by the lithium is picked up by another element. This element uses it to help fill its outer electron

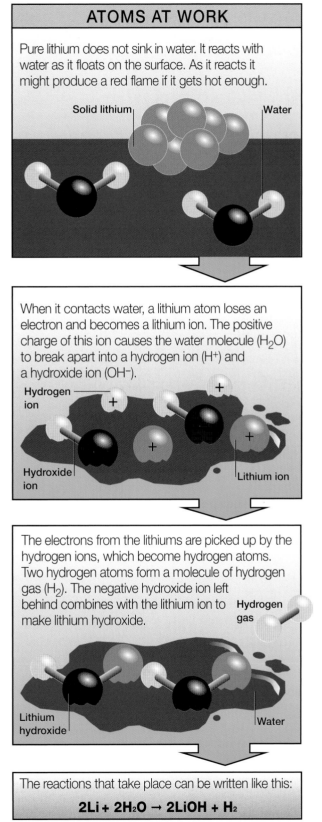

ATOMS AT WORK

Pure lithium does not sink in water. It reacts with water as it floats on the surface. As it reacts it might produce a red flame if it gets hot enough.

Solid lithium | Water

When it contacts water, a lithium atom loses an electron and becomes a lithium ion. The positive charge of this ion causes the water molecule (H_2O) to break apart into a hydrogen ion (H^+) and a hydroxide ion (OH^-).

Hydrogen ion

Hydroxide ion

Lithium ion

The electrons from the lithiums are picked up by the hydrogen ions, which become hydrogen atoms. Two hydrogen atoms form a molecule of hydrogen gas (H_2). The negative hydroxide ion left behind combines with the lithium ion to make lithium hydroxide.

Hydrogen gas

Lithium hydroxide

Water

The reactions that take place can be written like this:

2Li + 2H$_2$O → 2LiOH + H$_2$

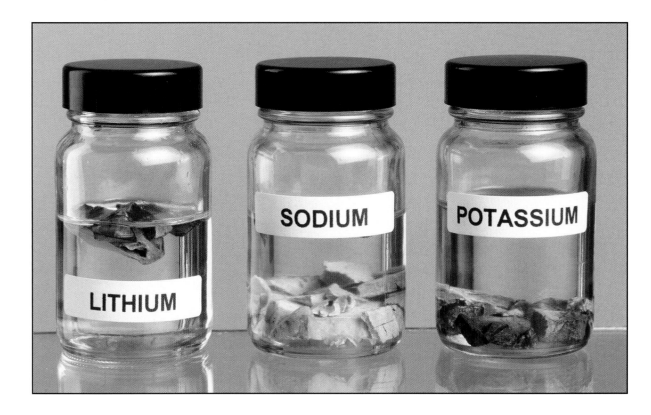

Lithium is less dense than other alkali metals and it floats in paraffin oil.

shell. For example, a chlorine atom has seven outer electrons and needs only one more to become stable. The chlorine atom picks up the lithium's electron and becomes a chloride ion with a charge of −1.

Because opposite charges attract each other, the positively charged lithium ion sticks to the negatively charged chloride ion. This is called ionic bonding.

Acids and alkalis

The reason why lithium is called an alkali metal is that it forms alkaline compounds when it combines with other elements. An alkali is the opposite of an acid. When an acid and alkali are mixed, they react violently and produce compounds that are neither alkaline or acidic. Chemists describe this process as neutralization.

Acids are very reactive compounds. Some are so reactive that they will destroy or eat away almost all solid objects. All acids contain hydrogen ions (H^+). These make the compound react easily with most substances. Stronger acids contain more hydrogen ions than weaker ones. Strong alkalis contain a lot of ions that will react with the hydrogen ions.

Lithium alkalis

The most alkaline lithium compound is lithium hydroxide (LiOH). This is produced when pure lithium reacts with water (H_2O). Lithium hydroxide is soluble, so it dissolves in water. As it dissolves it splits into lithium ions and hydroxide ions (OH^-).

When acid is added to the water, the acid also breaks into ions. A hydrogen ion and hydroxide ion combine to form water. The lithium ion bonds with the other ion left over from the acid to form a compound called a salt.

The most common salt in nature is sodium chloride (NaCl), which is called common salt. Chemists describe the other compounds produced by acid–alkali reactions as salts, too.

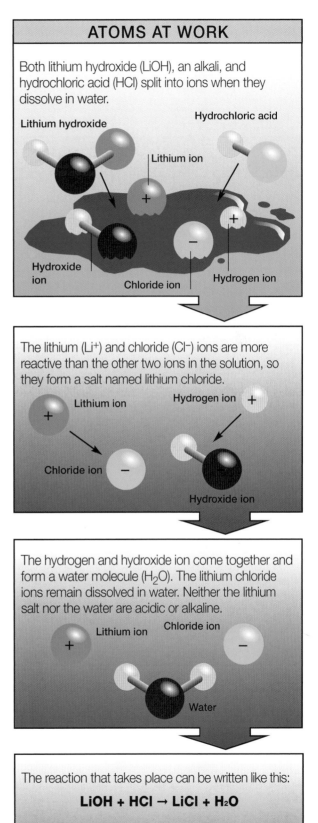

ATOMS AT WORK

Both lithium hydroxide (LiOH), an alkali, and hydrochloric acid (HCl) split into ions when they dissolve in water.

Lithium hydroxide

Hydrochloric acid

Lithium ion

Hydroxide ion

Chloride ion

Hydrogen ion

The lithium (Li^+) and chloride (Cl^-) ions are more reactive than the other two ions in the solution, so they form a salt named lithium chloride.

Lithium ion

Hydrogen ion

Chloride ion

Hydroxide ion

The hydrogen and hydroxide ion come together and form a water molecule (H_2O). The lithium chloride ions remain dissolved in water. Neither the lithium salt nor the water are acidic or alkaline.

Lithium ion

Chloride ion

Water

The reaction that takes place can be written like this:

$$LiOH + HCl \rightarrow LiCl + H_2O$$

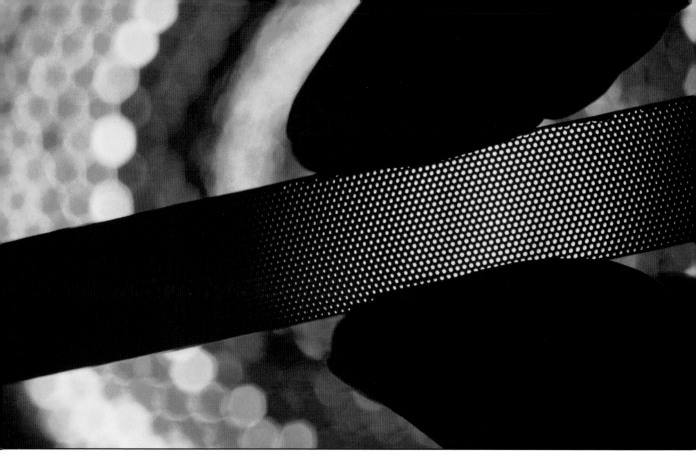

Uses of lithium

Lithium and it compounds have many uses. It is used to make powerful batteries that power laptop computers and cell phones. The metal is also an important ingredient in lightweight alloys used to make aircraft.

Some lithium compounds are used in soaps and greases. Others are used to dry air that blows through air-conditioners and to take gases out of the air inside spacecraft. Lithium is used in powerful hydrogen bombs. Lithium-containing crystals are also used to control lasers and to convert radio waves into electricity.

A strip of miniature lenses is made from lithium silicate glass. The lenses are the size of a human hair and are used in autofocus cameras.

Lithium alloys

An alloy is a mixture of metal atoms. By mixing different metals, chemists can make metals with very useful properties. Because lithium is so light, it is mixed with metals such as aluminum, copper, and cadmium to make strong but very light metal for items like aircraft.

Lithium is often alloyed as part of the purification process. Chlorides of the other metals in the alloy may be added to the melted lithium chloride. Atoms of these extra metals form at the same time as the lithium. The metal atoms mix into the pool of pure lithium in very exact amounts. Sometimes, the cathode contains certain metal atoms, which mix into the liquid lithium that forms.

Lithium is also used to purify other atoms. Because lithium is so reactive it is used to remove impurities in steel (a mixture of iron and carbon) and other alloys. The lithium removes unwanted elements, such as chlorine and sulfur.

Absorbers

Several lithium compounds are used to absorb unwanted substances from the air. For example, lithium chloride (LiCl) and lithium bromide (LiBr) are used in some air-conditioning systems. The compounds take the water vapor out of the hot air produced by the system. Lithium chloride and bromide are used in air-conditioners as strong brines. A brine is water that has a lot of salts dissolved in it. (Seawater is a natural brine, for example.)

Lithium hydroxide is used to absorb an unwanted gas as well. This time, the compound takes carbon dioxide (CO_2) out of the air. Carbon dioxide gets into the air when animals, including humans,

exhale. They get rid of the carbon dioxide because it is poisonous in large amounts. Usually the carbon dioxide gets blown away and does not build up to dangerous levels. However, in an enclosed space, such as a submarine or spacecraft, carbon dioxide can slowly build up. This makes it hard for the people onboard to breathe.

A shuttle astronaut replaces the canisters in the carbon dioxide scrubbers onboard a space shuttle. The scrubbers use lithium hydroxide to remove carbon dioxide from the air inside the spacecraft.

ATOMS AT WORK

Carbon dioxide (CO_2) gas in the air is pumped over lithium hydroxide (LiOH) crystals. The crystals have a little bit of water inside them to help the reaction.

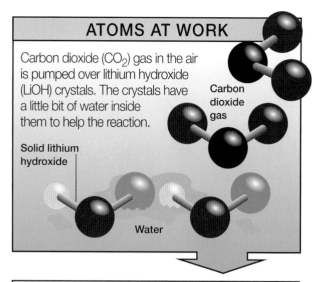

Solid lithium hydroxide

Carbon dioxide gas

Water

The lithium hydroxide breaks into ions. The hydroxide ion splits again. The oxygen joins the carbon dioxide to make a carbonate ion (CO_3^{2-}) and hydrogen joins another hydroxide ion to form a molecule of water (H_2O).

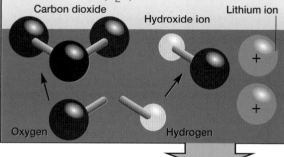

Carbon dioxide · Lithium ion · Hydroxide ion · Oxygen · Hydrogen

The lithium ion combines with the carbonate to form lithium carbonate. This dissolves in the water molecules produced.

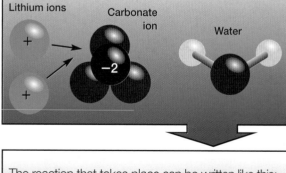

Lithium ions · Carbonate ion · Water

The reaction that takes place can be written like this:

$$2LiOH + CO_2 \rightarrow Li_2CO_3 + H_2O$$

Machines called scrubbers are used to take the carbon dioxide out of the air so people can breathe normally. Scrubbers contain lithium hydroxide pellets. The air is pumped over the pellets and the lithium hydroxide reacts with the carbon dioxide to form lithium carbonate and water. The pellets are gradually used up and must be refilled regularly.

Lasers and radars

Lithium forms a very useful compound called lithium niobate ($LiNbO_3$). This also contains oxygen and the very rare metal niobium. Lithium niobate forms clear crystals with unusual properties.

When light shines through a crystal of lithium niobate it is bent slightly. This effect is called refraction. The same effect produces rainbows and mirages and is also why a drinking straw often appears to bend when it is put in water.

The difference with lithium niobate is that when the crystal is electrified, it bends the light even more. The stronger the current, the more the crystal refracts light. This makes lithium niobate useful for controlling lasers.

The crystal is also useful for converting sound waves into electric signals. When the crystal is electrified it also vibrates in a way that produces sound. Lithium niobate crystals are used in radar systems and radio communication.

DID YOU KNOW?

FUSION BOMBS

The process that powers the Sun and other stars is called nuclear fusion. At the center of most stars, huge forces push hydrogen atoms together until they fuse together making helium atoms and a lot of heat and light. The very largest stars fuse heavier elements together to make even heavier atoms. All elements in nature have been made by stars in this way. The most powerful bombs ever invented use lithium to harness the power of nuclear fusion.

Thermonuclear bombs also fuse hydrogen atoms together and produce an enormous explosion. The bomb contains a small atomic bomb made of uranium or another radioactive metal. When this bomb explodes, it produces a lot of heat and streams of neutrons. These neutrons hit a supply of radioactive lithium hydride (LiH). This compound contains a lot of lithium-6 (Li 6) atoms, a rare isotope of lithium. Much of the hydrogen in the compound is deuterium, a radioactive isotope also called hydrogen-2 (H 2). The neutrons cause the Li 6 atoms to break down into tritium atoms. Tritium is another radioactive isotope of hydrogen, sometimes called hydrogen-3 (H 3). Under the force produced by the first explosion, the tritium atoms fuse with the deuterium atoms causing an even larger explosion. Thermonuclear weapons have never been used in war.

The first fusion bomb was tested by the United States in 1952 on a remote Pacific island. Fusion bombs are often called H-bombs because of the hydrogen isotopes they contain.

Lithium in batteries

One of the main uses of lithium is in batteries. Batteries are self-contained power supplies. Lithium batteries are very powerful for their size. Tiny lithium batteries are used in watches and pacemakers—a heart-rate controller used by people with heart problems. These small batteries cannot be recharged and have to be replaced regularly.

Larger lithium batteries can be recharged. They are used in portable devices that need a lot of electricity for a long time, such as video cameras, cell phones, and laptop computers.

How a battery works

A battery is a device that converts the energy of a chemical reaction into a current of electricity. They are set up in a similar way to the electrolysis system used to purify elements. However, the current flows in the opposite direction.

In a battery, there are two electrodes. The electrodes are separated by an electrolyte. The electrolyte is a substance that contains ions. Batteries only produce electricity when they are connected to a circuit. An electric circuit is a made up of metal conductors—usually wires—that connect the battery's two electrodes together. The circuit generally also contains something that uses electricity, for example, a light bulb.

Moving ions

In most batteries, the electrolyte is a liquid that contains ions. Once the circuit is connected, the ions in the electrolyte give up electrons to one of the electrodes. These electrons flow into the circuit as an electric current. At the other electrode, electrons flow into the electrolyte. This completes the flow of electrons, which continues to move through the battery and around the circuit. Eventually the ions in the electrolyte begin to run out, and the current becomes weaker.

Lithium batteries are small, but powerful and long-lasting. This is a rechargeable lithium-ion battery.

Many modern cell phones use lithium-ion batteries. These batteries are smaller than other types so that the phones can be smaller, too.

Some batteries can be recharged by running an electric current through them from another source. The current moves through the battery in the opposite direction from the current produced by the battery. This has the effect of reversing the reaction that took place in the battery as it made electricity. The ions are restored and the battery works again.

Using lithium

Lithium batteries are more complicated than most batteries. Because lithium is so reactive many liquid electrolytes will react with the pure lithium in the battery. The most common non-rechargeable lithium battery has one electrode made from solid lithium. The electrolyte and cathode in these batteries are actually a mixture of two liquids. One of these liquids contains sulfur, oxygen, and chlorine. The other is made up of lithium, chlorine, and aluminum. The lithium does not react with these liquids because a protective layer of lithium chloride forms on the surface of the metal.

ATOMS AT WORK

As a lithium-ion battery is charged, a current of electrons flows from the lithium oxide electrode to the carbon electrode. Inside the battery, lithium ions move through the separator to the carbon cathode.

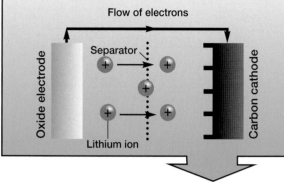

The carbon electrode collects the ions and gives them an electron so they become atoms. Once the battery is charged, the lithium atoms are stored in the carbon electrode untill the battery is used.

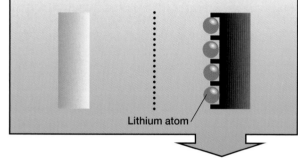

When the battery is in use, the lithium atoms in the carbon electrode release electrons. These electrons form the electric current produced by the battery. The lithium ions move from the carbon electrode back across the separator to the oxide electrode. When the lithium atoms in the carbon crystals run out the battery must be recharged.

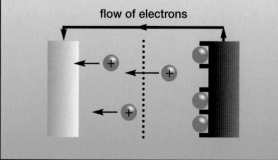

Rechargeable

Rechargeable lithium batteries are called lithium-ion batteries. They are made in a different way from the non-rechargeable ones. A lithium-ion battery does not have a liquid electrolyte. Instead the two electrodes are divided by a solid separator. One electrode is made of solid lithium oxide, often mixed with other metals, such as cobalt or manganese. This electrode is attached to a carbon current-collector. The other electrode is made of carbon.

When the lithium battery is being charged, lithium atoms in the oxide electrode give away electrons and become ions. The lithium ions pass through the separator to the carbon electrode. There the ions receive electrons and become atoms again. These atoms are stored in tiny spaces inside the electrode's crystals.

When the battery produces a current, the lithium atoms in the carbon electrode lose electrons and become ions once more. The electrons released become part of the electric current produced by the battery. The ion moves back across the separator to the lithium oxide electrode. There it picks up an electron and becomes a lithium atom. The electrons used to do this are supplied to the electrode by the current running from the carbon electrode. Once all the lithium atoms have moved back from the carbon electrode, the battery needs to be recharged.

Lithium and life

Unlike many other elements, lithium is not thought to be necessary for good health. However, it is found in tiny amounts in the body. This is because there are very small amounts of lithium compounds in the soil. These compounds are absorbed by the roots of plants. When animals, including humans, eat plants, the lithium compounds move into their bodies.

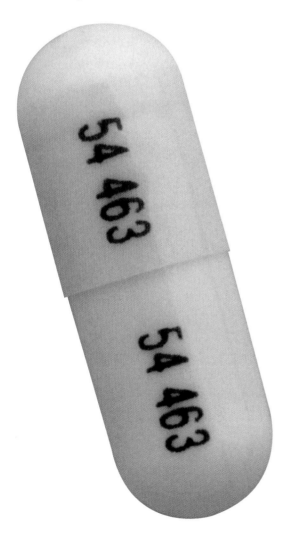

Too much lithium

Lithium poisoning is very rare because it rarely gets into food in large amounts. However, people with high blood pressure have to eat food without much salt in it. (The salt used in food is made up of sodium chloride.) People with only small amounts of sodium in their body are more at risk of being poisoned by lithium compounds in their food.

People with lithium poisoning feel sick and have stomach problems. They have skin problems and swollen ankles. Lithium also attacks the nervous system causing forgetfulness and trembling.

Lithium medicine

People suffering from certain mental illnesses take lithium carbonate. This compound helps control a person's moods, though doctors do not understand exactly how it works.

Lithium carbonate is used by people with bipolar disorder, which is sometimes called manic depression. People with this illness suffer from long periods of depression —or sadness—followed by a period of mania. People going though a manic phase may be very excited, agitated, or they may see things that are not there.

A small capsule contains a tiny amount of lithium carbonate. Some people with certain mental illnesses take these pills.

Periodic table

Everything in the universe is made from combinations of substances called elements. Elements are made of tiny atoms, which are too small to see. Atoms are the building blocks of matter.

The character of an atom depends on how many even tinier particles called protons there are in its center, or nucleus. An element's atomic number is the same as the number of protons.

Scientists have found around 116 different elements. About 90 elements occur naturally on Earth. The rest have been made in experiments.

All these elements are set out on a chart called the periodic table. This lists all the elements in order according to their atomic number.

The elements at the left of the table are metals. Those at the right are nonmetals. Between the metals and the nonmetals are the metalloids, which sometimes act like metals and sometimes like nonmetals.

- On the left of the table are the alkali metals. These have just one outer electron.

- Metals get more reactive as you go down a group. The most reactive nonmetals are at the top of the table.

- On the right of the periodic table are the noble gases. These elements have full outer shells.

- The number of electrons orbiting the nucleus increases down each group.

- Elements in the same group have the same number of electrons in their outer shells.

- The transition metals are in the middle of the table, between Groups II and III.

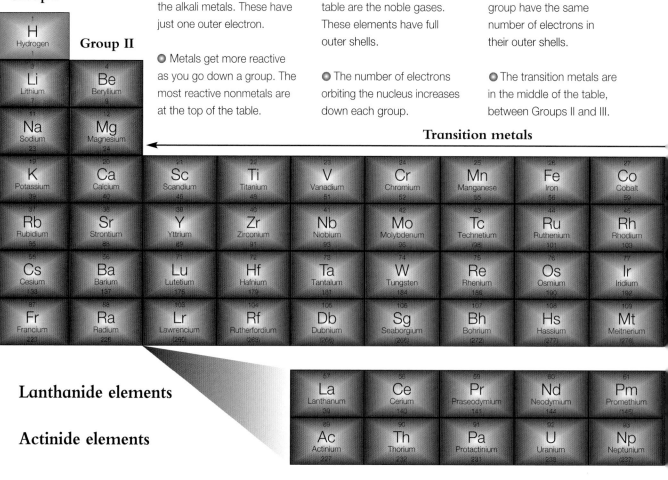

Group I

Group II

Transition metals

Lanthanide elements

Actinide elements

The horizontal rows are called periods. As you go across a period, the atomic number increases by one from each element to the next. The vertical columns are called groups. Elements get heavier as you go down a group. All the elements in a group have the same number of electrons in their outer shells. This means they react in similar ways.

The transition metals fall between Groups II and III. Their electron shells fill up in an unusual way. The lanthanide elements and the actinide elements are set apart from the main table to make it easier to read. All the lanthanide elements and the actinide elements are quite rare.

Lithium in the table

Lithium is in Group I. This group is called the alkali metals. Lithium is very reactive because it has just one electron in its outer shell. By losing this electron, it becomes more stable as a lithium ion. Nearly all lithium compounds are ionic. Lithium often forms alkali compounds. Alkalis are compounds that neutralize acids.

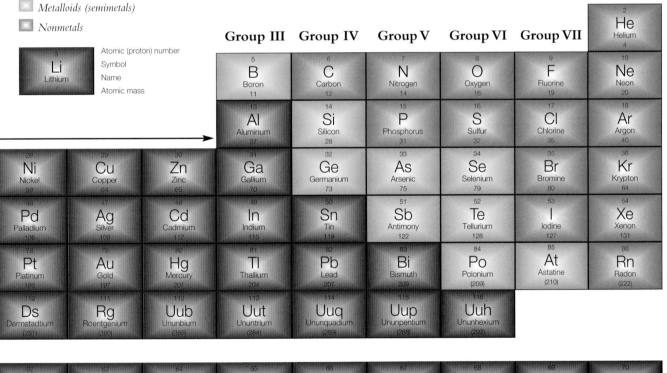

Chemical reactions

Chemical reactions are going on around us all the time. Some reactions involve just two substances, while others involve many more. But whenever a reaction takes place, at least one substance is changed.

In a chemical reaction, the atoms stay the same. But they join up in different combinations to form new molecules.

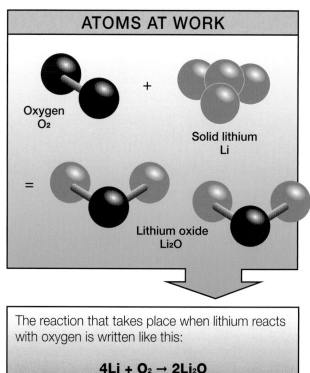

ATOMS AT WORK

Oxygen
O_2

Solid lithium
Li

Lithium oxide
Li_2O

The reaction that takes place when lithium reacts with oxygen is written like this:

$$4Li + O_2 \rightarrow 2Li_2O$$

Writing an equation

Chemical reactions can be described by writing down the number or atoms and molecules before and after the reaction. Since the atoms stay the same, the number of atoms before will be the same as the number of atoms after. Chemists write the reaction as an equation. This shows what happens in the chemical reaction.

Making it balance

When the numbers of atoms on both sides of the equation are equal, the equation is balanced. If the numbers are not equal, something is wrong. So the chemist adjusts the number of atoms involved until the equation balances.

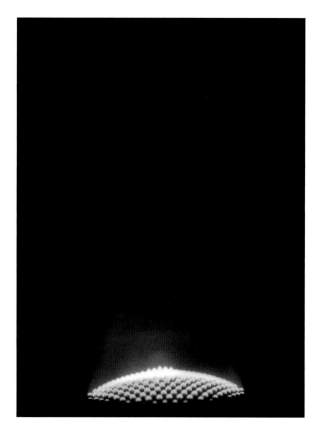

Lithium burning with a red flame is caused by a reaction between lithium and oxygen in the air to form lithium oxide.

Glossary

acid: An acid is a chemical that releases hydrogen ions easily during reactions.

alkali: A compound that neutralizes an acid producing water and a salt.

alkali metal: A group of elements that produce alkali compounds. Lithium is one of the alkali metals.

atom: The smallest part of an element having all the properties of that element.

atomic mass number: The number of protons and neutrons in an atom.

atomic number: The number of protons in an atom.

bond: The attraction between two atoms, or ions, that holds them together.

compound: A substance made of atoms of two or more elements. The atoms are held together by chemical bonds.

crystal: A solid consisting of a repeating pattern of atoms, ions, or molecules.

electrode: A material through which an electrical current flows into, or out of, a liquid electrolyte.

electrolysis: The use of electricity to change a substance chemically.

electrolyte: A liquid that electricity can flow through.

electron: A tiny particle with a negative charge. Electrons are found inside atoms, where they move around the nucleus in layers called electron shells.

element: A substance that is made from only one type of atom. Lithium is one of the alkali metals.

ion: An atom or a group of atoms that has lost or gained electrons to become electrically charged.

mineral: A compound or element as it is found in its natural form in Earth.

metal: An element on the left-hand side of the periodic table.

molecule: A unit that contains atoms held together by chemical bonds.

nuclear reactor: A machine that controls a nuclear reaction happening inside it.

nucleus: The dense structure at the center of an atom. Protons and neutrons are found inside the nucleus of an atom.

neutron: A tiny particle with no electrical charge. Neutrons are found in the nucleus of almost every atom.

ore: A mineral or rock that contains enough of a particular substance to make it useful for mining.

proton: A tiny particle with a positive charge. Protons are found in the nucleus.

reaction: A process in which two or more elements or compounds combine to produce new substances.

salt: A compound produced when an acid and alkali react. The most common salt is sodium chloride, which is the salt used to flavor food.

solution: A liquid that has another substance dissolved in it.

Index